Jennie Finch
Softball Superstar

Volume 1

Jennie Finch
Softball Superstar

Volume 1

Biography by
Christine Dzidrums & Leah Rendon

CREATIVE MEDIA, INC.
PO Box 6270
Whittier, California 90609-6270
United States of America

www.CREATIVEMEDIA.NET

Cover and Book design by Joseph Dzidrums
Cover photo by Joseph Dzidrums

First Edition: February 2013

Library of Congress Control Number: 2012914355

ISBN 978-1-938438-13-4   10 9 8 7 6 5 4 3 2 1

Love to Mom & Dad
The most supportive softball fans a daughter could ever have
-Christine

~~~~~~~~~~~~~~~~~~~~~~~~

Love to my family
The best Dodger fans in the world.
-Leah

Table of Contents

*"I was born and raised
a Dodger fan."*

DODGER DREAMS

"Jennie, time for baseball!" Bev Finch called.

Four-year-old Jennie Finch loved hearing those magical words. They meant that her family was heading to her favorite place in the world: Dodger Stadium.

Moments later the young girl fidgeted excitedly while her father Doug drove the Finch family up the 5 Freeway en route to Chavez Ravine where the Los Angeles Dodgers baseball team played all their home games. The tiny baseball fan grinned widely when she arrived at the stadium with her parents and older brothers, Shane and Landon. Jennie loved so many things about Dodger Stadium: the scent of Dodger Dogs cooking on the grill, the loud whacking noise that reverberated throughout the ballpark as players took batting practice and the excited chatter of 50,000 fans anticipating a thrilling game.

Jennie especially liked when the starting lineup featured her favorite pitcher, Orel Hershiser. The Cy Young winner and three-time All-Star had established the Major League record for most consecutive scoreless innings pitched when he went 59 innings without giving up a run. Jennie watched Bulldog, as he was nicknamed, with awe and admiration. She often wondered how it might feel to be such a dominant pitcher!

The Finches usually sat behind third base every game. Like many true blue Dodger fans, they brought a portable radio into the park, so they could listen to Hall of Fame sports-

Dodger Stadium was a Finch family tradition.
(Connie Dzidrums)

caster Vin Scully call each play. The Finch family attended many Dodger games over the years. Bev and her co-workers had pooled together resources to become proud season ticket holders.

One December afternoon, the Finches were trying to select a family Christmas card to send out that holiday season. Suddenly, the youngest family member came up with a bright

idea. Why not make Dodger Christmas cards? So that winter, relatives and friends of the Finch family received a very special baseball card!

Even years later, long after Jennie had become a major sports star, she remained a devoted Dodger fan. When asked by a reporter to name her favorite baseball team, she answered simply, "I bleed blue."

"Looking back now that I'm older, I realize sports has taught me: teamwork, sacrifice, leadership and dealing with failure and success."

Chapter One

T-BALL

Born on September 3, 1980, in La Mirada, California, Jennie epitomized the Southern California girl through and through. When baseball season ended, she turned her support toward her favorite basketball team, the Los Angeles Lakers. Among the team's star-studded lineup, the avid sports fan most admired point guard Magic Johnson.

Blessed to live in a warm climate, Jennie spent much of her childhood years outdoors. She loved soaking up the sun's warm rays while she played a variety of sports. She enjoyed simply watching sporting events, too, frequently attending her brothers' Little League baseball games. Although, truth be told, the youngster could hardly wait for the day when she would have the opportunity to play organized sports.

Despite her love of sports, Jennie wasn't necessarily a tomboy. She liked her share of girly activities, too. One could often spot her sitting quietly on her bedroom floor surrounded by a large assortment of Barbies. She would lovingly brush her dolls' long, golden tresses and dress them in pink or black, her favorite colors.

Shortly after Jennie turned five, her parents surprised her with the best birthday present ever. Doug and Bev Finch signed their energetic daughter up for the L'il Miss T-Ball League. Jennie's bright eyes lit up with joy when her mother and father took her shopping for her first baseball glove and aluminum bat.

On Jennie's first day of t-ball practice, it became quite evident that she possessed natural athletic talent. Not only did the sturdy little girl with blonde pigtails easily outrun all her teammates, she could also fire a ball with amazing power and precision.

On the exciting day that the girls ordered their uniforms, Jennie insisted on wearing #3. Los Angeles Dodger Steve Sax, the popular second baseman with blinding speed, also wore that number. A thrill shot through Jennie when she slipped on her freshly pressed uniform. For the first time, she felt like a real ballplayer!

At age seven, Jennie switched from t-ball to fast pitch softball. Instead of hitting the ball off a tee, pitchers were integrated into the game. As the strongest and tallest girl, Jennie volunteered to pitch for her team and discovered she was good at it. Not only could she throw the ball all the way to home plate, she did so with surprising power and control. A pitcher was born!

Whether she was pitching or hitting, Jennie adored playing softball. She loved so many aspects of the sport: the uniform, playing outdoors, getting dirty and even eating post-game snacks. Most of all, she loved the competitive part of softball. She thrived on winning games. If her team lost, she became angry and the disappointment inspired her to work harder during the next practice. More than anything, Jennie hated second place.

Buoyed by his daughter's enthusiasm, Jennie's father became her personal pitching coach and equipment supplier. Doug always ensured that his young ballplayer had adequate training materials. He built a batting cage in the backyard of their home so she could practice her swing anytime. He also

Jennie was born in La Mirada, California.
(Joseph Dzidrums)

constructed a pitch-back out of a trampoline for the nights he was not home to catch for her, even drawing batter outlines in chalk.

Not surprisingly, Jennie developed a deep bond with her father, who worked as a cement truck driver. She often approached him when struggling with a softball-related problem or personal issues. Plus, no one made her laugh like her dad!

Jennie had a strong relationship with her mother, as well. Bev worked hard as secretary at an outpatient surgery unit in their hometown to help provide for her family. Nevertheless she always took time off from work to attend her children's sporting events. The devoted mother even kept a detailed score book of every softball game her daughter played.

Like most young girls, Jennie enjoyed expressing her femininity. She braided colorful ribbons into her golden hair on every game day. The fashionista also sported glittery headbands, a tradition she continued throughout her entire career. She even liked splashing on perfume before a game. After all, why not smell like a million bucks while playing hard?

By the time Jennie reached age nine, she established herself as one of the best softball players in her age group. In fact, thanks to her strong talent, she joined a traveling All-Star team that played games across Southern California. Every weekend the excited youngster traveled to a new, exciting city for the sole purpose of playing her favorite sport! Suddenly, softball played a bigger role in her life than she initially envisioned.

"It hit me," she later recalled "'I could be good at this and it could take me far.'"

Jennie's talent appeared evident to everyone. Family, friends and even strangers repeatedly approached Doug and

Bev Finch to rave about the youth's special talent. The humble parents just smiled and thanked everyone for their praises. They felt extremely proud of their daughter's accomplishments but they still considered softball merely a fun hobby. Even so, it was becoming clear that the sport had become a huge part of their lives.

"My family vacations were softball tournaments," Jennie later told *The Washington Times*. "The sacrifices [my parents] made growing up, understanding what they did for me and seeing the benefits I have from it, it's amazing."

Around the same time, Doug developed an astonishing invention that he named the Finch Windmill. The exercise/training device strengthened shoulder muscles without its users actually needing to pitch. The youngest Finch credited the equipment with improving her pitching in regard to speed, accuracy, muscle balance and muscle memory.

At age twelve, Jennie and her All-Star team, the California Cruisers, qualified for the national championship title. The excited tween and her teammates flew all the way to Chattanooga, Tennessee, to compete for American Softball Association's ultimate prize. In the end, the Southern California girls showed remarkable skill and confidence in winning the championship.

After the game, Jennie beamed with pride as she clutched her shiny trophy. Nothing brought her greater satisfaction than earning a victory after a hard-fought game. She loved softball with all her heart.

"I loved school. I loved the social atmosphere, and I loved competing."

Chapter Two

THE HIGH SCHOOL YEARS

In 1994 Jennie began her freshman year at La Mirada High School. The teenager felt excited to spend the next four years as a Matadore. Although she played travel ball, she looked forward to the challenge of high school softball, too.

In her first year at La Mirada High, Jennie easily made the varsity softball team. The fourteen-year-old felt great pride when she wore her blue and gold uniform and battled other high schools for softball supremacy.

Jennie was, of course, her team's star pitcher. She thrived on holding the ball during crucial games. The versatile also played shortstop and packed a powerful punch as a hitter, too.

Jennie also became interested in volleyball and basketball. At first, she felt too bashful to try out for either sport. After all, she owned a strong reputation as an outstanding softball player. What would people think if she wasn't as good at volleyball and basketball? After thinking it through, though, Jennie chose to ignore the insecurity clouding her mind. The prospect of playing new sports seemed enticing. If she wasn't the best player on the team, so what? She would still enjoy herself.

And as it turned out, Jennie excelled at volleyball and basketball, too. In fact, during her senior year, she was voted captain and MVP of her volleyball, basketball and softball squads!

La Mirada Matadores
(Joseph Dzidrums)

Playing two new sports brought several bonuses into Jennie's life. She made friends with several nice girls that she would have never met otherwise. Moreover, she realized that volleyball and basketball benefitted her physically, too. She became quicker on her feet and attained stronger flexibility. Soon her softball performances featured improved agility.

In addition to being highly involved in extracurricular activities, Jennie always made time for a social life, too. Friendships were highly important to her, and she felt especially close to two twin sisters named Jasmine and Bianca. The three best friends nicknamed themselves the Bomb Squad and could always be found laughing up a storm as they ate together during lunch hour. Sometimes after school they would go shopping or hang out in front of a television watching shows like *Beverly Hills, 90210* or *Saved By the Bell* reruns. The Bomb Squad would remain good friends after high school, too.

A good student, Jennie maintained a strong grade point average. The focused teenager's hard work helped her remain eligible for after-school sports. Although math was her least favorite subject, she always enjoyed attending her Spanish class.

Around the same time, Jennie began eyeing college opportunities. Having established a solid reputation on the high school and traveling team levels, several top universities courted the star pitcher to play for their school.

"I started realizing there were college scholarships out there, and it could pay for my way," she said. "I started watching those college teams and becoming interested in them."

When Jennie was 14 years old, she arrived home from school one day to discover she had received her first letter of interest from a university. UCLA contacted her and expressed

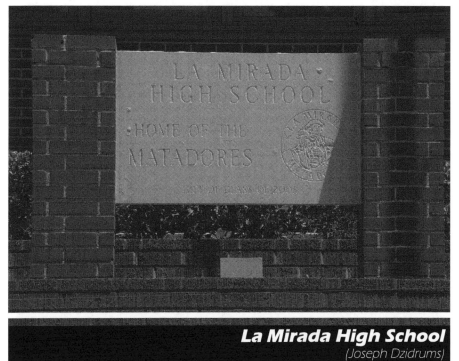

La Mirada High School
(Joseph Dzidrums)

hope in staying in touch. The Bruins' attention felt especially neat since the teenager had been their bat girl many years earlier. Before long, a steady stream of letters arrived from universities across the country! Jennie always placed the letters in a special box with the knowledge that someday she would make a very important decision about her educational future.

Sometimes softball's hard work exhausted Jennie. She spent 35 hours a week on her sport. On a few occasions she dreamed of a more traditional childhood instead.

"Why can't I be normal?" she asked her folks.

"We're a softball family; we're not normal," her dad replied.

Softball remained close to Jennie's heart, though. Her high school sports career thrived. By her senior year, she delivered six perfect games, 13 no-hitters and a 0.15 ERA.

Sometimes Jennie slyly used her softball talent to her advantage off the field. She had eyed a gold and silver Guess

La Mirada High's Softball Field
(Joseph Dzidrums)

La Mirada High's Scoreboard
(Joseph Dzidrums)

watch for some time. One evening Bev drove her daughter home after she'd just finished pitching a perfect game. Suddenly the teenager turned to her mom with a mischievous smile.

"Can I get the watch if I pitch another perfect game?" she asked.

Bev Finch mulled over the idea. Her youngest child was a good student who never caused trouble. Okay, if Jennie pitched another perfect game, she could have the watch. Sure enough, the teen threw a perfect game at her next opportunity.

"I rocked that Guess watch," the star later laughed.

When Jennie was 15 years old, softball debuted as an official medal sport at the 1996 Summer Olympics in Atlanta, Georgia. Led by Dot Richardson and Lisa Fernandez, Team USA won the gold medal over second place finishers China. Jennie watched the Atlanta Games with unbridled enthusiasm.

Earlier that year, her parents drove her to Mayfair Park (later renamed Lisa Fernandez Field) in nearby Lakewood to watch the team play. She watched her idols carefully, absorbing how they trained, played and prepared. Afterwards she even waited in line to get Fernandez and Laura Berg's autographs.

Golden Smile
Glenn Harris/PR Photos

"Mom and Dad, that's what I want to do," she said on the drive home. "I want to play Team USA softball."

Months before graduation, the moment arrived for Jennie to choose a college. Most universities clamored to sign the star player for their team. Except Jennie had already set her heart on playing for University of Arizona. Many of her teammates from her travel team, the Batbusters, attended school there. Plus, she considered Arizona head coach Mike Candrea like a second father. One of softball's greatest coaches, he had led University of Arizona to several national championships.

"Coach Candrea has a way of bringing out the best in his players," Jennie told the *Arizona Desert Swarm*. "You want so very badly to perform for him and for Arizona softball and the rich tradition that he's built there. He's so great at finding what each athlete needs as an individual but yet he does it in that team atmosphere and really getting the best out of everybody."

Nevertheless, Bev insisted that her daughter entertain other college offers. Jennie eventually accepted two recruitment visits. She first toured the University of Washington campus and fell in love with the natural beauty of the campus. However, when she visited University of Arizona several weeks later, the educational institution simply felt like home to her. She committed to the college on the second night of her trip.

When high school graduation finally arrived, Jennie looked back on her career with few regrets. La Mirada High School named her Female Athlete of the Year, and the *Long Beach Press-Telegram* awarded her Player of the Year. She had conquered high school softball. Bring on college!

"When you step on campus, every Wildcat's goal is not to get to the College World Series - it's to win it."

Chapter Three

UNIVERSITY OF ARIZONA

Heading into a major softball school, like University of Arizona, as a top ranked recruit certainly carried lofty expectations. This was not lost on the smart teen who thrived on the pressure.

"The teams that I played on were always successful," Jennie remarked. "Winning becomes a regularity. Second place isn't good enough. When we'd lose, it was a big shock. You'd think, 'Oh my gosh! We're not supposed to lose. I'm not used to losing.' So coming into a top program helps. When I entered, they had five National Championships, so you want that tradition; you want that pressure on you. It's a good challenge coming into one of the top elite programs."

However, moving away from home was a major adjustment for the college freshman. At first, she struggled to adapt to changes in her softball training and daily routines.

"It was a definite change being away from home and under a new environment," she recalled. "The whole atmosphere: four to five hours on the field, two hours in the weight room, and strengthening, conditioning, and running. You definitely have to prioritize your time. You live with two other girls your same age and there's no curfew. So it's definitely a big adjustment."

Overall, though, Jennie felt happy with her decision to become a Wildcat. It was a thrilling day when she received her red and blue uniform and practice gear. She loved hanging out with the athletic department and felt like part of a close-knit family.

Freshman year started a bit shakily for Jennie who split her time between first base and pitching. For starters, she faced stronger batters who could hit her pitches. She also felt disappointment at being the team's number two pitcher. It had been years since Jennie wasn't the top pitcher on her team. She missed holding the ball during crucial game moments.

In later years, Jennie always wore #27.

La Mirada Girl Makes Good
Koi Sojer/PR Photos

"As a freshman, you want to come in and make an impact," she told the *Arizona Star.* "You don't want to have to sit the bench. You want to be in there and perform."

Her disappointment led her to make changes in her approach to the game. She began the grueling process of refining her various pitches: fastball, curve ball, screwball, drop ball and rise ball. The strategy paid off remarkably, and the hard-working pitcher ended the season with a strong 24-6 record.

Another softball milestone occurred that year when Jennie was invited to try out for the Junior National team. The nervous teen flew to the Olympic Training Center in San Diego with big dreams of earning the privilege to represent her country in competition. At the end of the tryout, officials chose Jennie as one of 17 girls for the team.

Right away, Jennie represented USA at the Junior World Championships in Taipei, Taiwan. Not only did the American girls handily win the competition, the other players treated them as rock stars. The opposing teams noticed that the American girls wore beautiful uniforms and played with higher-quality equipment and gear.

Following that assignment, Jennie was promoted to the Senior National Team. Among her new teammates? The legendary Lisa Fernandez, widely considered the greatest softball player of all time. Lisa had represented UCLA in collegiate softball and was a key member of Team USA for many years. Jennie couldn't believe she was playing alongside her hero!

As a member of the U.S. National Team, Jennie soaked up the travel opportunities that accompanied her assignments. She saw countries she might never have had the chance to

Jennie reveals a softer side.
(Joseph Dzidrums)

visit otherwise, including exciting locations like Brazil, Japan, Venezuela and the Dominican Republic. However, Jennie's favorite part of each trip involved wearing her softball uniform with USA emblazoned across the chest.

Meanwhile, Jennie's second season as a Wildcat eclipsed her first. The determined pitcher posted an astonishing 29-2 record with a 0.79 ERA. She even collected three no-hit games in the post season, although Arizona narrowly missed playing in the championship game.

The following season Jennie felt determined to lead her team to a victory at the Women's College World Series. She performed remarkably well all season posting an undefeated record of 29-0. Meanwhile, she had a strong defensive and offensive team behind her.

When the Wildcats finally faced the UCLA Bruins in the championship game, Lindsey Collins scored the game's lone run with a home run in the fourth inning. Meanwhile, Jennie handled the pitching pressure with the confidence of a steady veteran. Pitching a shutout game with seven strikeouts, Jennie led her team to a 1-0 victory, earning MVP honors for her outstanding efforts. She didn't hesitate when asked to recall her favorite memory from the championship game.

"Obviously the last pitch and feeling that excitement with those other eight seniors," she said. "They would have been the first class to not win a world series in their four years at Arizona, so there was a lot of pressure for them. Sending them out on top was the greatest feeling. All my hard work, all my hours spent, all my parents' time, effort and money that they put into it. They get you to college but your next step is winning a national championship. It's the greatest feeling. It's what gets you up at 5 a.m. to work out and strive to be better."

Despite losing the championship title, the Bruins displayed strong sportsmanship by praising the more dominant team. After all, they had lost to the Wildcats four times that season.

"I tip my cap to Arizona," UCLA coach Sue Enquist told *The Associated Press.* "They did what they had to do. When they got their one opportunity, they took a swing at it and they got it."

Jennie closed out her senior year at University of Arizona in historic fashion. Resuming her dominating ways from her junior season, she posted wins and inched toward the record books. Florida State's Rebecca Aase held the record for most consecutive victories by a college pitcher with 50. On February 24, 2002, Jennie arrived at her home stadium to see fans packing the stands for her team's game against Cal State Northridge. If Jennie won that Sunday's game, she would net her 51st victory, setting a new NCAA record.

As Jennie warmed up for the game, she glanced at the crowd watching her every move. Some fans sported #51 shirts, while chants of "51" reverberated throughout the park.

When Jennie took the mound, spectators cheered her wildly. The focused athlete pitched her usual stellar game, taking her team to a 6-0 victory and setting a college record in the process. Months later, Jennie would finally cap off the impressive accomplishment with 60 straight victories.

"Obviously, the undefeated season was right behind my ear," she remarked. "I'm sure my team got sick of hearing it.

It was this whole thing of Jennie's streak, so it was a relief in a way when it was over. But after that season, it was more about just doing my job on the mound and putting up a W for my team."

"Rebecca Aase, I don't want to take anything away from her, but they play a little different schedule than we play," Coach Candrea told *The Arizona Daily Star*. "It's pretty phenomenal, considering what (Jennie) had to go through to get here. It's hard to do."

"(Jennie) is pretty relaxed, and she keeps things on the low," teammate Lisha Ribellia added. "She is pretty humble, so she's not one to brag."

University of Arizona made it back to the College World Series in 2002. Once again, Coach Candrea handed the ball to his star pitcher in the final championship game. Unfortunately, despite a well-fought game by Jennie and her teammates, University of California, Berkeley walked off with the big win.

Although Jennie felt crushed by her team's loss, the school's cheering section embraced their star athlete. The well-educated softball fans knew that Jennie had played a major role in their team's success all season. As the distraught pitcher left the mound, the spectators showered her with a prolonged standing ovation. Their heartfelt gesture elicited a tiny smile from the overwhelmed pitcher.

"Jennie Finch is why we got here," Coach Candrea later praised.

Devastated by her loss in the final collegiate game of her career, a teary Jennie sat stunned for several minutes in the dugout. When the 6'1" athlete finally rose to leave the field, she noticed an enormously large crowd had assembled in the outfield area. It turned out that adoring fans were waiting patiently for her autograph!

Although Jennie's NCAA career had ended, her college days were not quite over. She remained in Arizona an additional year to complete her communications degree. During this time, she also worked as a volunteer assistant coach for the University of Arizona softball team. The insightful athlete especially enjoyed passing down her sports knowledge to the next generation of Wildcats.

Less than a year after completing her astonishing NCAA career, Jennie received a tremendous honor. On May 9, 2003, University of Arizona retired her number 27 jersey. The ceremony took place at 6:45 p.m., just before a much-anticipated game between Arizona and UCLA. The popular player also threw out the ceremonial first pitch.

"This is an incredible moment," an emotional Jennie told the packed crowd. "I told myself I wasn't going to cry but here they come."

That the accolade occurred right before Jennie's graduation seemed fitting. The beloved pitcher would forever hold University of Arizona dear to her heart, but she was leaving to conquer other parts of the world now. Her college days had officially ended but her career was just taking off!

"It's really kinda shocking to me. No one in our sport has ever really gotten this kind of attention."

Chapter Four

OPPORTUNITIES

Not long before Jennie graduated from University of Arizona, an encounter changed her life. One day Major League Baseball's Luiz Gonzalez brought his rising-star teammate Casey Daigle to a Wildcats game. The younger player became instantly smitten with the college pitcher.

A few weeks later, an unassuming Jennie arrived at her hair salon and was greeted by five dozen roses, along with a date request from her suitor. Casey had used his amateur detective skills to discover her next appointment. Shortly afterward, the two athletes began dating.

The new couple came from drastically different backgrounds. Jennie was a big city girl from the Los Angeles area, while Casey grew up on a farm in Louisiana. Still they were crazy about each other and shared one very important thing: strong family values. Jennie felt certain she'd met her soul mate in Casey and considered herself very blessed.

Meanwhile, with the Olympics less than two years away, Jennie's profile skyrocketed. The public clamored to learn more about the softball superstar who would provide a bright presence at the 2004 Athens Olympics.

Most notably, the pitcher became the first female correspondent on the long-running TV series, *This Week in Baseball*. In her segment, entitled "Pitch, Hit, and Run with Jennie Finch," she interviewed Major League Baseball players on the fundamentals of the game. In some instances, she even pitched to the mega stars, striking out the Angels' Scott Spiezio, the Dodgers' Paul Lo Duca, the Colorado Rockies' Larry Walker and the Seattle Mariners' Mike Cameron.

"She struck me out on three pitches," Lo Duca told the *Los Angeles Times*. "She's nasty. I caught her in the bullpen, and I could barely catch it."

San Francisco Giant Barry Bonds stood watching the action with great interest. The perennial All Star would one day set the all-time Major League Baseball home run record. Finally, he approached softball's most famous pitcher and a well-known Dodger fan

"I heard you're one of the best," he remarked. "Well, you're not the best until you face the best."

"You haven't faced my riseball," Jennie shot back.

In the end, Barry stood in the batter's box but refused to swing his bat. Meanwhile, superstar Alex Rodriguez watched from the sidelines. He, too, chose not to face the imposing pitcher.

"I was very surprised, very impressed by it," Alex told the *Albany Times Union*. "It would be a challenge for anybody, even a big-league player."

"It's been amazing," Jennie gushed. "It's been such a thrill. There's been so much excitement meeting these people I've always looked up to and watched play. I'm able to meet with them, hang out with them, and pick their brain. That's what every softball player wants. Their dream is to be able to play the game of softball for their living and they're doing it."

Jennie
FINCH

the SHOWDOWN

the DELL
DIAMOND

AUGUST
12-15
—2010—

Jennie vs. Cat

NATIONAL PRO FASTPITCH

Jennie headlines a National Pro FastPitch ad.

"I grew up going to Dodger games," she laughed. "But never would I believe that I would be on the field pitching to some of the players, and walking in the dugout, and hanging out and meeting Tommy Lasorda. It's a dream come true."

"It's been great," she added. "Most of them have seen me on the College World Series and they know of me, so it's always fun going into an environment where they have respect for you. They want to know just as much about softball and pitching as I want to know about baseball and the life of a major leaguer. One funny remark was 'How do you throw the ball so hard?' It's just funny seeing them react to a girl that can actually strike them out, and I've had the opportunity to do that, so it's been fun."

Jennie eagerly embraced her role as softball ambassador. The popular athlete believed her high-profile appearances generated incredible exposure for her sport, so she accepted as many promotional opportunities as possible. She attended the *ESPY Awards*, appeared on *NBC's Today Show* and even chatted with late night television host David Letterman.

With her collegiate career behind her, Jennie was no longer bound by NCAA rules and could accept financial rewards for endorsement deals. Thanks to her softball success and exceptional good looks, advertisers swarmed the softball star with offers. Jennie signed contracts with several companies, but she remained levelheaded regarding the celebrity side of life.

"It's not my goal for Jennie Finch to be a household name," she remarked. "My goal is to win the gold medal."

Jennie did sign a high-profile deal with Mizuno, though. The athletic equipment company unveiled a pink line of Jennie

Jennie walks the red carpet.
Lee Roth/PR Photos

Finch gear including: batting gloves, bats, clothing apparel and cleats. Now young softball players could dress like their hero!

Jennie also dabbled in the broadcasting booth by doing commentary on *ESPN* for the College World Series. The athlete quickly realized that play-by-play analysis was much harder than it appeared.

"It was a good experience," she remarked. "I was really raw at the whole thing, coming in with no experience in the broadcasting area. It's a different view of the game. I didn't realize how much work went into commentary. It was an overwhelming week, but it was fun."

As Jennie's professional life thrived, her personal life reached an all-time high. One evening Casey blindfolded his girlfriend and led her to the pitching mound at Rita Hillenbrand Memorial Stadium at University of Arizona. He then got down on one knee and proposed, and she accepted.

"He blindfolded me and said we were going to dinner," she told *Modern Bride*. "We got to the field where he'd first seen me throw. He walked me out to the mound. There were gerbera daisies and champagne on a blanket, and he was on one knee. He had the ring in a ceramic box in the shape of a baseball and he said, 'You've been the queen of the diamond for four years, and I want you to be the queen of my heart.'"

Family and friends reacted enthusiastically to the duo's engagement. However, the young couple opted to have a long engagement. Casey was still adapting to life as a professional baseball player, while Jennie had a little event called the Athens Olympics just a few months away.

Forever a Pitcher
(Joseph Dzidrums)

"Every time I put my uniform on, wearing Team USA across my chest, there's no greater feeling than that."

Chapter Five

2004 ATHENS OLYMPICS

The U.S. Girls' Softball team entered the Athens Olympics as the overwhelming favorites to take the title. The American women had never lost the Olympic gold medal, and they were expected to cruise to a third straight victory.

"You're coming into the United States of America softball team," Jennie remarked before Athens. "They've won two gold medals. Nothing less is better. As far as my role goes, I want to do everything possible for me to be the best that I can be for the team and play whatever role that may be in grace."

Jennie couldn't shake the surreal feeling that she would soon be playing in the Olympics with women she had idolized for so long. Just eight years earlier, she waited in line for the autographs of Lisa Fernandez and Laura Berg. Now those legends were her teammates!

Mike Candrea, Jennie's coach at University of Arizona, would lead Team USA. The beloved and respected man felt honored to guide the talented group of women toward the Olympic podium. He expressed constant awe at his roster.

"They're probably the best team I've ever seen," he gushed. "And I think it will go down in the Olympic legacy, and people will talk about it for a long time."

Sadly, tragedy struck shortly before the Athens Games, when Coach Candrea's wife Sue died suddenly after experienc-

ATHENS 2004

ing a brain aneurysm. A mother figure to many girls on the U.S. team, the stunned, grief-stricken players banded together and dedicated their Olympics to the woman they loved so dearly.

"(Coach Candrea's) a strong man, next to my father the strongest man I know," Jennie told the *Tucson Citizen*: "And he is like a father to us. We know he's going to have that void in his heart, but she'll be right there and we'll play for Sue. She wouldn't have wanted it any other way (but for him to coach). I don't know anyone who wanted us to beat up the opponents more than her, wanting us to bring home the gold."

Thanks to a heavy schedule, Team USA landed in Athens several weeks before the start of the games. In fact, the Athlete's Village wasn't even ready yet. Every day the women watched organizers slowly build the village piece by piece until it was finally ready to welcome the world's top athletes.

A few days before the start of the games, Coach Candrea informed an emotional Jennie that she would be the starting pitcher in the United States' first game, where they would face Italy. The young Olympian felt enormously humbled to be entrusted with such a huge honor.

When Jennie arrived at the Olympic Softball Stadium in the Helliniko Olympic Complex for game one, she'd never seen a more perfect ballpark in all her life. Nestled along the Aegean Sea, the stadium's beauty, flanked by the symbolic Olympic rings, nearly brought tears to her eyes.

Mere seconds before taking the field for the start of the game, Jennie gave herself an internal pep talk. Though she felt more nervous than she'd ever felt in her life, the well-conditioned athlete reminded herself that, in the end, she was playing just another softball game. The motivational talk worked and she pitched exceptionally well against the first few batters she faced.

Unfortunately, disaster struck in the third inning when Jennie tore an oblique muscle during a pitch. Rather than risk aggravating the injury, team doctors immediately pulled her from the game to begin treatment on her strain.

Despite the physical setback, Jennie started a game against Canada a few days later. Fighting through enormous pain, she turned in a heroic performance, pitching a one-hitter and leading her team to another victory. Throughout the entire ordeal, she kept her injury a secret from the media, preferring to keep the focus solely on Team USA's quest for a third straight gold medal.

The American-Canadian showdown turned out to be Jennie's final game in Athens. Her injury prevented her from pitching in any future games at those Olympics. Meanwhile, a phenomenal Lisa Fernandez took on the lion's share of the pitching.

Rather than wallow in self-pity about her injury, Jennie displayed exceptional sportsmanship by becoming an active participant on the sidelines, cheering on her teammates during each play in every game. Her teammates felt thankful for her positive presence in the dugout.

Team USA faced Australia in the gold medal match. The Americans cruised to the title with a 5-1 victory. Tears of pride filled Jennie's eyes as Olympic officials draped a gold medal around her neck. Moments later she experienced goose bumps when the "Star-Spangled Banner" played over the stadium's sound system.

"You dream of that moment forever," she later recalled. "To be able to be up there with my role models, and to have my family there, and see our flag raise, and the "National Anthem" play, there was nothing like that."

Growing up, the plucky kid from La Mirada had imagined that gold medal ceremony nearly every day of her life. In Athens, she realized that with hard work and determination, life-long dreams could come true.

Olympic Champion
(Richard Yaussi)

"I love being outside with my boys, playing tag or trying to keep up with them."

Chapter Six

LIFE CHANGES

Jennie started the new year with a bang. She and Casey were married on January 15, 2005, at the historic Crystal Cathedral in Garden Grove, California. The bride wore a Maggie Sottero "Cinderella" ball gown, while the groom, groomsmen, and bridesmaids donned elegant black.

Of course, guests weren't surprised when the ceremony featured a baseball theme. The ring bearer wore a black "Daigle" jersey with Casey's baseball number, and the flower girl walked down the aisle in a white "Finch" baseball jersey

The Crystal Cathedral
(Joseph Dzidrums)

Jennie and Casey
(Glenn Harris/PR Photos)

with Jennie's softball number. In addition, the bride's something borrowed and something blue came in the form of an Arizona garter belt given to her by a friend.

After the ecstatic couple exchanged vows, they headed to a wedding reception in Santa Ana with 200 of their closest friends and family. Two days later, the blissfully happy pair left for a romantic honeymoon in the South Pacific, where they shut off their cell phones, relaxed and even swam with sharks.

When Jennie returned home she began training for the National Pro Fastpitch, the only professional women's softball league in the United States. In December of 2004, she signed a one-year contract with a new expansion team, the Chicago Bandits, who would play their home games at Benedictine University in Lisle, Illinois. Her teammates included Olympian Leah O'Brien-Amico and All-American Jaime Clark.

Team USA
(Bob Charlotte/PR Photos)

We are extremely excited to add Jennie to the roster," said Bill Conroy, the Chicago Bandits owner. "She is an extraordinary athlete, a great role model for young girls and is the foundation on which you can build a franchise and ultimately a league."

"To be able play professionally and play in one of the great sports towns there is -- Chicago -- is amazing," Jennie told *The Herald News*. "Our fans have been tremendous and the media's support has been tremendous. We're leading the pack and hopefully we are the example for all the other teams. It's fun to be able play the game we love day in and day out professionally."

"You only live once," she added. "Play while you can."

In her first year on the Bandits, Jennie made the All-Star team and earned Co-Pitcher of the Year honors. She also post-

Jennie in a television commercial for Chobani.
(Chobani)

A Reflective Jennie
(Joseph Dzidrums)

ed a .88 ERA and 144 strikeouts. A strong offensive player as well, she hit .309 with 22 RBIs and six home runs.

When the popular player eventually ended her career with the team in 2010, the organization responded by retiring her jersey number. In addition, after the Chicago Bandits moved their stadium to Roseville, the city's mayor announced the new address as 27 Jennie Finch Way.

"To be honored this way is nothing short of amazing," an emotional Jennie responded. "I am so grateful to have been a

Jennie models her new medal.
(Bob Charlotte/PR Photos)

Bandit and to have played softball professionally in the NPF (National Pro Fastpitch)."

In September of 2005, Jennie received life-altering news when she discovered that she and Casey were expecting a child. Not only was the mother-to-be thrilled with the news, she also remained adamant that she would return to softball following the birth of her baby. The determined athlete still planned to compete at the world championships in China the following summer. Plus, it was never too early to start thinking about the 2008 Beijing Olympics.

The fit athlete remained active throughout her pregnancy. On May 4, 2006, Jennie's life was changed for good when her son Ace entered the world. Right away, motherhood had a profound effect on her.

"As a mom, a piece of your heart is removed and in this little human being, and you want everything to be so perfect for them," she told *iVillage.com.*

After giving birth, the new mom had just six weeks to prepare for tryouts for the world championships team. Shortly after her son turned two weeks old, Jennie flew home to California with her newborn and began training intensively with her father. Her hard work and dedication paid off when she made the team.

Ace saw a large part of the world for the next few months. He traveled everywhere with his mother: Canada, San Diego and Oklahoma. He even accompanied Mom to China for the world championships, which Team USA won.

In early 2008, Jennie appeared as a contestant on *The Celebrity Apprentice.* Rather than competing for an apprenticeship with Donald Trump, like on the regular version of the show, the celebrities competed for a charity. The famous pitcher selected the Breast Cancer Research Foundation but was eliminated early on in the competition.

Two years later, the U.S. Women's Softball team returned to China for the Beijing Olympics. It was a bittersweet time for the sport's best players, though. Earlier, the International Olympic Committee had voted to eliminate softball from Olympic competition. 2008 Beijing would mark the final time the games would feature softball.

Once again, the Americans were huge favorites to claim gold. As usual, they got off to a remarkable start. When it came time for the championship game against Japan, though, the United States stumbled ever so slightly. In a stunning upset, Japan won the gold medal, while the Americans settled for silver. Although Jennie appeared clearly devastated by the loss, she put the disappointment into perspective.

"Wearing this uniform, you're used to winning," she told *Access Hollywood*. "But you know in the end, yes, we have a silver medal and a lot of people would dream about that."

On July 26, 2010, Jennie and her teammates faced Japan again at the World Cup of Softball. This time the Americans tasted redemption when they defeated their rivals 5-1.

Jennie played first base in the championship game. The number 27 was printed on the base bag. Every American woman wore glitter headbands. When Jennie was lifted from the game in the seventh inning, she received a thunderous standing ovation from the crowd as she walked off the field – for good.

After ten years, Jennie was retiring from the sport. Though the esteemed athlete still played at the top of her game, she had grown weary of the travel and time away from her family. After years of being at the center of the softball community, she wanted to focus on her own family.

"I think sometimes you measure a person's success not on their accomplishments as much as how many lives they've touched," Coach Candrea told *USA Today* after the game. "Jennie has transformed this sport, touched millions of young kids in many different ways — whether it's fashion, whether it's the way she plays the game — but through it all she's been very humble."

"She's become the face of this sport, and not many people could do that," he added. "It's hard to do."

"She's become an ambassador for our sport," U.S. teammate Leah O'Brien-Amico told *The Washington Times*. "She's well-spoken. She's beautiful. And she does her talking on the field. Everything she's gotten is well-deserved."

Immediately following the game, Jennie remained on the field for over an hour as she signed autographs for her many admirers. It was important to her to honor every fan request. After all, she had made a public vow to encourage others to continue playing and promoting the sport. Maybe waiting in the sea of autograph seekers was a hopeful young girl who dreamed of someday becoming the next Jennie Finch.

When asked to sum up her softball experience, Jennie's response featured a mixture of wistfulness and awe.

"Amazing," she said breathlessly. "Way beyond anything that I could ever possibly imagine. It was an incredible journey."

The legend retired with the comforting knowledge that she had helped establish softball as a respected sport The superstar had exposed a whole new generation of girls to the game.

"When I was growing up, softball had stereotypes along with other female sports," she remarked. "Society is changing. Muscles on female athletes are okay. Young girls can look up to beautiful, athletic, fit women."

On June 19, 2011, Jennie and Casey became parents for a second time with the birth of their son, Diesel Dean. Four months after giving birth, the mother of two ran in the New York City Marathon.

On January 12, 2013, Jennie and her husband welcomed their daughter Paisley Faye into the world. The proud parents would encourage their child to be athletic, independent and strong. Like her brothers, the youngest Daigle would pursue her dreams, whatever they may be.

To this day, Jennie still campaigns with the hope of getting softball restored as an Olympic sport. She hosts various softball camps across the United States and even runs the Jennie Finch Softball Academy in Flemington, New Jersey.

Mostly, though, Jennie enjoys spending time with her family. Like her parents did for her, Jennie encourages her children to get involved in physical activity.

And on many afternoons in the Daigle household, one can sometimes hear Mom call out those eight magical words.

"Ace, Diesel and Paisley, it's time for baseball!"

Team USA Highlights

2010 World Champions
2010 World Cup Champions
2010 All NPF Team
2010 NPF Regular Season Champions
2009 World Cup Champions
2009 Japan Cup Champions
2008 Silver Medalist at 2008 Olympic Games
2007 Gold Medalist at Pan American Games
2007 World Cup Champions
2006 Gold Medalist at ISF World Championships
2006 World Cup Champions
2005 Silver Medalist at Japan Cup
2005 Silver Medalist at World Cup
2004 Gold Medalist at 2004 Olympic Games
2003 Gold Medalist at Pan American Games
2002 World Champions

2012 ESPY Awards
Koi Sojer/PR Photos

Jennie's Favorites

Favorite Movie
A League of Their Own

Favorite Color
Pink

Favorite Bread
Wheat

Favorite School Subject
Spanish

Favorite Ethnic Food
Cajun

Favorite Junk Food
Cheez-Its

Favorite Music
Country

Favorite Card Game
Canasta

Favorite Hobby
Shopping

Favorite Bible Verse
"I can do all things in Christ who gives me strength".

Favorite Clothing Item
Sweatpants.

Favorite Indulgence
Pedicures

About the Authors

Christine Dzidrums holds a bachelor's degree in Theater Arts from California State University, Fullerton. She previously wrote the biographies: *Joannie Rochette: Canadian Ice Princess, Yuna Kim: Ice Queen, Shawn Johnson: Gymnastics' Golden Girl, Nastia Liukin: Ballerina of Gymnastics, The Fab Five: Jordyn Wieber, Gabby Douglas and the U.S. Women's Gymnastics Team,* and *Gabby Douglas: Golden Smile, Golden Triumph.* Her first novel, *Cutters Don't Cry,* won a 2010 Moonbeam Children's Book Award in the Young Adult Fiction category. She also wrote the tween book, *Fair Youth,* and the beginning reader books, *Timmy and the Baseball Birthday Party* and *Timmy Adopts a Girl Dog.* Christine also authored the picture book, *Princess Dessabelle Makes a Friend.* She recently competed her second novel, *Kaylee: The 'What If ?' Game.*

Leah Rendon graduated with a Bachelor of Arts degree from the University of California, Los Angeles. She coauthored the children's sports' biographies *Joannie Rochette: Canadian Ice Princess, Shawn Johnson: Gymnastics' Golden Girl* and *Jennie Finch: Softball Superstar.* The Southern California native also contributed to the tween book, *Fair Youth.*

Build Your SkateStars™
Collection Today!

At the 2010 Vancouver Olympics, tragic circumstances thrust **Joannie Rochette** into the international spotlight when her mother died two days before the ladies short program. The world held their breath for the bereaved figure skater when she competed in her mom's memory. Joannie then captured hearts everywhere by courageously skating two moving programs to win the Olympic bronze medal.
Joannie Rochette: Canadian Ice Princess profiles the popular figure skater's moving journey.

Meet figure skating's biggest star: **Yuna Kim**. The Korean trailblazer produced two legendary performances at the 2010 Vancouver Olympic Games to win the gold medal in convincing fashion. *Yuna Kim: Ice Queen*, the second book in the **Skate Stars** series, uncovers the compelling story of how the beloved figure skater overcame poor training conditions, various injuries and numerous other obstacles to become world and Olympic champion.

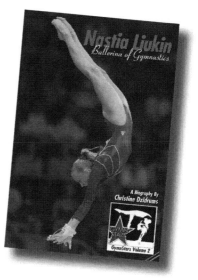

Shawn Johnson, the young woman from Des Moines, Iowa, captivated the world at the 2008 Beijing Olympics when she snagged a gold medal on the balance beam.

Shawn Johnson: Gymnastics' Golden Girl, the first volume in the **GymnStars** series, chronicles the life and career of one of sport's most beloved athletes.

Widely considered America's greatest gymnast ever, **Nastia Liukin** has inspired an entire generation with her brilliant technique, remarkable sportsmanship and unparalleled artistry.

A children's biography, *Nastia Liukin: Ballerina of Gymnastics* traces the Olympic all-around champion's ascent from gifted child prodigy to queen of her sport.

2010 Moonbeam Children's Book Award Winner! In a series of raw journal entries written to her absentee father, a teenager chronicles her penchant for self-harm, a serious struggle with depression and an inability to vocally express her feelings.

"I play the 'What If?'" game all the time. It's a cruel, wicked game."

Meet free spirit Kaylee Matthews, the most popular girl in school. But when the teenager suffers a devastating loss, her sunny personality turns dark as she struggles with debilitating panic attacks and unresolved anger. Can Kaylee repair her broken spirit, or will she forever remain a changed person?

Meet **Princess Dessabelle**, a spoiled, lonely princess with a quick temper. When she orders a kind classmate to be her friend, she learns the true meaning of friendship.

Build Your Timmy™
Collection Today!

Meet 4½ year old Timmy Martin! He's the biggest baseball fan in the world.

Imagine Timmy's excitement when he gets invited to his cousin's birthday party. Only it's not just any old birthday party... It's a baseball birthday party!

Timmy and the Baseball Birthday Party is the first book in a series of stories featuring the world's most curious little boy!

Timmy Martin has always wanted a dog. Imagine his excitement when his mom and dad agree to let him adopt a pet from the animal shelter. Will Timmy find the perfect dog? And will his new pet know how to play baseball?

Timmy Adopts A Girl Dog is the second story in the series about the world's most curious 4½ year old.

Twelve-year-old Emylee Markette has felt invisible her entire life. Then one fateful afternoon, three beautiful sisters arrive in her sleepy New England town and instantly become the most popular girls at Forest Springs Middle School. To everyone's surprise, the Fay sisters befriend Emylee and welcome her into their close-knit circle. Before long, the shy loner finds herself running with the cool crowd, joining the track team and even becoming friends with her lifelong crush.

Through it all, though, Emylee's weighed down by nagging suspicions. Why were the Fay sisters so anxious to befriend her? How do they know some of her inner thoughts? What do they truly want from her?

When Emylee eventually discovers that her new friends are secretly fairies, she finds her life turned upside down yet again and must make some life-changing decisions.

Fair Youth: Emylee of Forest Springs marks the first volume in an exciting new book series.

Made in the USA
Middletown, DE
29 June 2018